Rock of Ages

A Worship and Songbook for Retirement Living

DISCIPLESHIP RESOURCES

P.O. BOX 340003 • NASHVILLE, TN 37203-0003
www.discipleshipresources.org

Credits

8 "Basic Pattern of Worship" © 1976 Abingdon Press; © 1980, 1984, 1989 The United Methodist Publishing House. Used by permission.

10, 12 "An Order for Morning Praise and Prayer" and "An Order for Evening Praise and Prayer" © 1989 The United Methodist Publishing House. Used by permission.

10, 12 "Prayer of Thanksgiving" in "An Order for Morning Praise and Prayer" and in "An Order for Evening Praise and Prayer" by Daniel T. Benedict, Jr. Used by permission.

14 "Memorial Service" adapted from "A Service of Death and Resurrection" in *The United Methodist Hymnal.* © 1989 The United Methodist Publishing House. Adapted by permission.

22, 23 Prayers from *The Book of Common Prayer* (Seabury Press, 1979).

25, 26 "A Service for Upholding a Resident Moving From Independent Living to Nursing Care" and "A Room Blessing for a New Resident" from *With Faces to the Evening Sun: Faith Stories From the Nursing Home,* by Richard L. Morgan. Copyright © 1998 by Richard L. Morgan. Used by permission of Upper Room Books.

28 "A Litany for Aging" from *1999 International Year of Older Persons: Resource Materials for Congregational Ministry With Older Adults,* by Richard H. Gentzler, Jr. © 1998 The General Board of Discipleship. Used by permission.

ISBN 978-0-88177-643-0

Printed in the United States of America

DR 643

Contents

Dedication

This book is dedicated to the countless pastors, chaplains, lay visitors, musicians, worship leaders, and other volunteers who spend many hours leading worship services and offering Christ's care and healing touch in nursing homes, assisted-living settings, retirement communities, hospitals, and homes. They provide joyful memories, loving presence, and hopeful futures for people not able to attend worship services in their home congregations.

Acknowledgment

We hope you enjoy using this collection of songs and worship resources. We believe that it will be useful for worship with older adults in long-term healthcare facilities, assisted-living settings, retirement communities, hospitals, and homes.

Rock of Ages was produced by the combined effort of many people. Dr. Julius A. Archibald, Jr., originally envisioned this book, and the United Methodist Committee on Older-Adult Ministries presented the concept to the General Board of Discipleship. Through the work of the Center on Aging and Older-Adult Ministries and the Center for Worshiping Resources, this resource became a reality.

We believe that older adults are God's gifts to us and that they continue to be members of the household of faith. Let us continue to learn from them, honor them, and work to ensure a healthy, happy quality of life for all. May we capture the sense of awe and wonder so many older adults have for our Lord Jesus Christ. May we have such faith as we worship with them using *Rock of Ages*.

Richard H. Gentzler, Jr.
Daniel Benedict
Dean McIntyre

Introduction for Use

What Is Here and Why

Throughout our lives we seek God and respond to the presence of the Holy One. Those who reach retirement years continue to practice patterns of worship and praise started earlier in life. Retirement and the perspective of age provide opportunity to deepen faith and to enter more fully into a life of prayer and service. Participation in corporate worship is an essential discipline that sustains, forms, and guides faithful discipleship.

Although many older adults continue to worship in local church settings, some are unable to do so. Others appreciate the opportunity to gather for worship with others with whom they eat, play, and live. This book was developed to provide a basic resource for those who plan worship and for those who gather for worship in retirement communities, convalescent hospitals, and other gatherings of older adults.

The worship resources in this book are in large type for ease of reading. Several orders of worship are included that are suited to retirement communities, nursing homes, and other similar settings.

The resources for worship are of two basic types: hymns and songs, and orders of worship and prayers. This book was developed by United Methodists and aims at use of orders, prayers, hymns, and songs that are familiar. At the same time, this book is intentionally ecumenical; and we hope that all Christians will adapt it for their use. The index gives the page numbers on which the hymns and songs are found not only in *The United Methodist Hymnal* but also in *The Baptist Hymnal*, *The Presbyterian Hymnal*, and the *Lutheran Book of Worship*.

This book has a basic order of worship for use on Sundays that can be used when Communion is celebrated or when it is not. An authorized person—someone ordained or otherwise set apart or recognized by a denomination for the ministry of Word and sacrament—should preside when Communion is celebrated.

The services for evening and morning are for use where people gather for daily prayer, marking the beginning and ending of any day of the week. If the basic order will be used on the Lord's Day (Sunday), then the morning or evening service may be used as an additional service. The services for morning and evening are not preaching services, so an ordained or authorized person is not required for leading such services.

The memorial service is for use when a death occurs in the retirement community. It may be used as the primary service if a funeral was not held elsewhere for the deceased, or it may be used as a service of remembrance and thanksgiving for the person when the primary funeral service was held at another time or location.

Planning and Leading Worship

The assumption of this book is that planners and leaders of worship may be people from within the retirement community who desire to plan and lead worship among themselves. In some situations, they may come from nearby local churches. The following paragraphs will help to orient those who use this resource to plan and lead worship. In addition, planners and leaders should review the rubrics (directions) at the top of each of the orders.

The hymns and prayers were selected with the calendar of the Christian year in mind. This is so that senior adults can participate with the larger church in keeping time with Christ and can share the praise and prayer of the whole church. Some senior adults may be familiar with the Christian calendar; others may need encouragement and instruction to appreciate its richness.

The primary anchor of our identification as Christians is our baptism and the covenant that God made with us by water and the Spirit. As such, all baptized Christians are marked as disciples and share in Christ's ministry. Worship should affirm the full dignity and participation of Christians. Planners and leaders should avoid actions that talk down to or in any way underestimate the gifts and contributions of each worshiper.

Almost all Christians are familiar with and appreciative of the Lord's Supper. The sacrament, as most Christians understand it, is a means of grace in which God is powerfully present to forgive, heal, liberate, and unify us as Christians with one another, both the living and the dead, and with God's own self. In some situations, it will be appropriate for every Lord's Day gathering to include Holy Communion. In others, it will be appropriate to celebrate Communion monthly or at some other interval. The retirement community should be consulted with and considered in deciding the frequency. If many or most of the people regularly participate in a local congregation, frequent celebration may be redundant.

Whenever Communion is celebrated, the table should be extended to those who cannot, for health or other reasons, be present. People who are able should be trained and sent with Communion elements to those who cannot be present. This action does not need to be carried out by ordained or otherwise specially authorized people, as it is taking what has already been blessed and shared by the community. Extending the table in this way should be done within a short time after the service. Elements should not be reserved or kept until another day.

Planners and leaders should feel free to supplement this book with resources from *The United Methodist Hymnal, The United Methodist Book of Worship,* or the corresponding hymnal and book of worship of the planner's denomination or of the retirement community's primary denominational constituency. Additional worship resources are available on the website of the Worship Resource Center of the General Board of Discipleship (www.gbod/worship).

Participation in song is both prayer and communion with God and one another. Often, the strongest connection to our past and to our deep emotions, memories, and yearnings is discovered and recovered in singing. Planners and leaders are encouraged to give careful thought and provision to support of the corporate song of the gathered community. While solos and other performances on behalf of the community are appropriate, they should never be done in ways that displace the ministry of all in offering a sacrifice of praise and thanksgiving. Strong accompaniment on piano or other instruments should be a priority.

Worship Resources

Basic Pattern of Worship

Gathering

The people come together in the Lord's name. There may be greetings, music and song, prayer and praise.

Proclamation and Response

The Scriptures are opened to the people through the reading of lessons, preaching, witnessing, music, or other arts and media. Interspersed may be psalms, anthems, and hymns. Responses to God's Word may include acts of commitment and faith with offerings of concerns, prayers, gifts, and service for the world and for one another.

Thanksgiving

In services with Communion, the actions of Jesus in the upper room are reenacted: taking the bread and cup, giving thanks over the bread and cup, breaking the bread, and giving the bread and cup.

In services without Communion, thanks are given for God's mighty acts in Jesus Christ.

Sending Forth

The people are sent into ministry with the Lord's blessing.

Services of Daily Prayer

From the earliest days of the church, Christian worshipers saw the rising of the sun and the lighting of the evening lamps as symbolic of Christ's victory over death. "An Order for Morning Praise and Prayer" and "An Order for Evening Praise and Prayer" enable United Methodists to celebrate daily the life, death, and resurrection of Jesus Christ.

These services focus on the praise of God and prayer for God's creation, rather than on the proclaiming of the Word. Therefore, preaching or other devotional talks are inappropriate in these services. When Scripture is used, passages should be chosen that will encourage the community in its praise and prayer.

Each order reflects a simple yet flexible pattern. The openings, hymns, songs of praise, responses to prayers, and Lord's Prayer may all be sung, with or without accompaniment. Scripture, silence, and prayer are optional.

Each order is to be celebrated in a community of Christians at various occasions in their life together. These orders may be used on any occasion when Christians gather, but they are not adequate substitutes for the full Sunday service of Word and Table.

Laity are encouraged to lead these services, and parts of the service may be led by different people.

The communal quality of prayer is emphasized when the people stand or sit in a circle facing one another. The setting may be simple, with a focus such as a cross or candle.

An Order for Morning Praise and Prayer

This service is for groups as they begin their day in prayer.

Call to Praise and Prayer

The following may be sung or spoken.

O Lord, open our lips.
And we shall declare your praise.

Morning Hymn

A hymn appropriate to the morning may be sung.

Prayer of Thanksgiving

The following or other prayer of thanksgiving may be said by the leader or by all:

God, whose Word echoes and resounds in all creation, you spoke and the universe came to be; you spoke again and the creation was made new in Christ. We rejoice to be and to believe. Let your word be upon our lips and in our hearts. Give yourself to others through us as in Christ you gave yourself for the world. **Amen.**

Scripture

Deuteronomy 6:4-9; Psalm 51, 63, or 95; Isaiah 55:1-3; John 1:1-5, 9-14; Romans 12:1-2; or other readings appropriate to the morning, or to the day or season of the Christian year, or to the nature of the occasion, may be used.

Silence

Silent meditation on the Scripture that has been read. This may be concluded with a short prayer.

Song of Praise

A Scripture song or hymn may be sung.

Prayers of the People

Intercessions for the world, the suffering, the church, and the communion of saints may be offered, with anyone voicing a brief prayer of intercession or petition. For forms of intercessions, see The United Methodist Hymnal *(page 877).*

The Lord's Prayer

See page 21 in this book.

Blessing

The grace of the Lord Jesus Christ, and the love of God, and the communion of the Holy Spirit be with you all. **Amen.**

The Peace

Signs of peace may be exchanged.

An Order for Evening Praise and Prayer

This service is for groups as they end their day in prayer.

Proclamation of the Light

A candle may be lit and lifted in the midst of the community. The following may be sung or spoken.

Light and peace in Jesus Christ.
Thanks be to God.

Evening Hymn

A hymn appropriate to the evening may be sung.

Prayer of Thanksgiving

The following or other prayer of thanksgiving may be said by the leader or by all:

God of our days and nights, we rejoice greatly in your mercy and nearness at the close of this day's journey. We thank you for tasks accomplished and for the inner peace to entrust unfinished things to your care. We thank you for a place to lie down in safety while you sustain the world in life. Even in the hush of falling asleep, may we contemplate your justice and joy at work in the world, through Jesus Christ, our Lord. **Amen.**

Scripture

Genesis 1:1-5, 14-19; Exodus 13:21-22; Psalm 23, 90, 121, 141; Matthew 25:1-13; Romans 5:6-11; 1 Thessalonians 5:1-10; Revelation 22:1-5; or other readings appropriate to the evening, or to the day or season of the Christian year, or to the nature of the occasion, may be used.

Silence

Silent meditation on the Scripture that has been read. This may be concluded with a short prayer.

Song of Praise

A Scripture song or hymn may be sung.

Prayers of the People

Intercessions for the world, the suffering, the church, and the communion of saints may be offered, with anyone voicing a brief prayer of intercession or petition. For forms of intercessions, see The United Methodist Hymnal *(page 879).*

The Lord's Prayer

See page 21 in this book.

Blessing

The grace of Jesus Christ enfold you this night.
Go in peace. **Thanks be to God.**

The Peace

Signs of peace may be exchanged, or all may depart in silence.

Memorial Service

If the primary service for the deceased will be held elsewhere, this service may be used. If the primary service for the deceased is to be held in the retirement community, make appropriate adaptations to the service.

ENTRANCE

Gathering

Music for worship may be offered. Hymns and songs of faith may be sung during the gathering.

The Word of Grace

Jesus said, I am the resurrection and I am life. Those who believe in me, even though they die, yet shall they live, and whoever lives and believes in me shall never die. I am Alpha and Omega, the beginning and the end, the first and the last. I died, and behold I am alive for evermore, and I hold the keys of hell and death. Because I live, you shall live also.

Greeting

Friends, we have gathered here to praise God and to witness to our faith as we celebrate the life of *Name*. We come together in grief, acknowledging our human loss. May God grant us grace, that in pain we may find comfort, in sorrow hope, in death resurrection.

Hymn or Song

Prayer

The following or other prayers may be offered, in unison if desired. Petition for God's help, thanksgiving for the communion of saints, confession of sin, and assurance of pardon are appropriate here.

O God, speak to us once more your solemn message of life and of death. Help us to live as those who are prepared to die. And when our days here are accomplished, enable us to die as those who go forth to live, so that living or dying, our life may be in you, and that nothing in life or in death will be able to separate us from your great love in Christ Jesus our Lord. Amen.

The following prayer of confession and pardon may also be used:

Holy God, before you our hearts are open, and from you no secrets are hidden. We bring to you now our shame and sorrow for our sins. We have forgotten that our life is from you and unto you. We have neither sought nor done your will. We have not been truthful in our hearts, in our speech, in our lives. We have not loved as we ought to love. Help us and heal us, raising us from our sins into a better life, that we may end our days in peace, trusting in your kindness unto the end; through Jesus Christ our Lord, who lives and reigns with you in the unity of the Holy Spirit, one God, now and for ever. Amen.

Who is in a position to condemn? Only Christ, Christ who died for us, who rose for us, who reigns at God's right hand and prays for us. Thanks be to God who gives us the victory through our Lord Jesus Christ.

Here Psalm 130 may be used.

PROCLAMATION AND RESPONSE

Old Testament Lesson

Psalm 23

See page 19 in this book. Sung or said by the people standing.

New Testament Lesson

Psalm, Canticle, or Hymn

Gospel Lesson

Sermon

A sermon may be preached, proclaiming the gospel in the face of death. It may lead into, or include, the following acts of naming and witness.

Naming

The life and death of the deceased may be gathered up by the reading of a memorial or appropriate statement, or in other ways, by the pastor or others.

Witness

Family, friends, and members of the congregation may briefly voice their thankfulness to God for the grace they have received in the life of the deceased and their Christian faith and joy. Signs of faith, hope, and love may be exchanged.

Hymn or Song

Creed or Affirmation of Faith

See page 20. If the creed has not been preceded by, it may be followed by, a hymn or musical response.

COMMENDATION

Prayers

The following prayer may be offered, or another prayer may be used. It may take the form of a pastoral prayer, a series of shorter prayers, or a litany. Intercession, commendation of life, and thanksgiving are appropriate here.

God of us all, your love never ends. When all else fails, you still are God. We pray to you for one another in our need, and for all, anywhere, who mourn with us this day. To those who doubt, give light; to those who are weak, strength; to all who have sinned, mercy; to all who sorrow, your peace. Keep true in us the love with which we hold one another. In all our ways we trust you. And to you, with your church on earth and in heaven, we offer honor and glory, now and for ever. **Amen.**

Here the presiding minister may commend the deceased and the gathering to God. The presiding minister may administer Holy Communion to all present who wish to share at the Lord's table. Otherwise, the service continues as follows:

Prayer of Thanksgiving

God of love, we thank you for all with which you have blessed us even to this day: for the gift of joy in days of health and strength, and for the gifts of your abiding presence and promise in days of pain and grief. We praise you for home and friends, and for our baptism and place in your church with all who have faithfully lived and died. Above all else we thank you for Jesus, who knew our griefs, who died our death and rose for our sake, and who lives and prays for us. And as he taught us, so now we pray.

The Lord's Prayer

See page 21 in this book.

Hymn

Dismissal With Blessing

Other Worship Resources

Psalm 23 (King James Version)

For sung responses, see The United Methodist Hymnal *(137).*

The LORD is my shepherd; I shall not want.
He maketh me to lie down in green pastures:
he leadeth me beside the still waters.
He restoreth my soul:
he leadeth me in the paths of righteousness
for his name's sake.
Yea, though I walk through the valley of the
shadow of death,
I will fear no evil: for thou art with me;
thy rod and thy staff they comfort me.
Thou preparest a table before me
in the presence of mine enemies:
thou anointest my head with oil;
my cup runneth over.
Surely goodness and mercy shall follow me
all the days of my life:
and I will dwell in the house of the LORD
for ever.

The Apostles' Creed

I believe in God the Father Almighty,
maker of heaven and earth;

And in Jesus Christ his only Son our Lord:
who was conceived by the Holy Spirit,
born of the Virgin Mary,
suffered under Pontius Pilate,
was crucified, dead, and buried;
the third day he rose from the dead;
he ascended into heaven,
and sitteth at the right hand of God
the Father Almighty;
from thence he shall come to judge
the quick and the dead.

I believe in the Holy Spirit,
the holy catholic* church,
the communion of saints,
the forgiveness of sins,
the resurrection of the body,
and the life everlasting. Amen.

**universal*

The Lord's Prayer

Our Father, who art in heaven,
hallowed be thy name.
Thy kingdom come,
thy will be done on earth as it is in heaven.
Give us this day our daily bread.
And forgive us our trespasses,
as we forgive those who trespass against us.
And lead us not into temptation,
but deliver us from evil.
For thine is the kingdom, and the power,
and the glory, forever. Amen.

Other Prayers

Advent

Merciful God, who sent your messengers the prophets to preach repentance and prepare the way for our salvation: Give us grace to heed their warnings and forsake our sins, that we may greet with joy the coming of Jesus Christ our Redeemer; who lives and reigns with you and the Holy Spirit, one God, now and for ever. **Amen.**

Christmas

Almighty God, we joyfully celebrate the birth of your only Son Jesus Christ. Grant that we, who have been made your children by adoption and grace, may be renewed each day by your Holy Spirit; through our Lord Jesus Christ, to whom with you be honor and glory, now and for ever. **Amen.**

Lent

O God, whose glory it is always to have mercy: Be gracious to all who have gone astray from your ways, and bring them again with penitent hearts and steadfast faith to embrace and hold fast the unchangeable truth of your Word, Jesus Christ your Son; who with you and the Holy Spirit lives and reigns, one God, for ever and ever. **Amen.**

Easter

Easter Day

Almighty God, who through your only-begotten Son Jesus Christ overcame death and opened to us the gate of everlasting life: Grant that we, who celebrate with joy the day of the Lord's resurrection, may be raised from the death of sin by your life-giving Spirit; through Jesus Christ our Lord, who lives and reigns with you and the Holy Spirit, one God, now and for ever. **Amen.**

Sundays of Easter

O God, whose Son Jesus is the good shepherd of your people: Grant that when we hear his voice we may know him who calls us each by name, and follow where he leads; who, with you and the Holy Spirit, lives and reigns, one God, for ever and ever. **Amen.**

Thanksgiving

Accept, O Lord, our thanks and praise for all that you have done for us. We thank you for the splendor of the whole creation, for the beauty of this world, for the wonder of life, and for the mystery of love.... Grant us the gift of your Spirit, that we may know Christ and make him known; and through him, at all times and in all places, may give thanks to you in all things. **Amen.**

New Year's Eve/Day

A Covenant Prayer in the Wesleyan Tradition

I am no longer my own, but thine.
Put me to what thou wilt,
rank me with whom thou wilt.
Put me to doing, put me to suffering.
Let me be employed by thee
or laid aside for thee,
exalted for thee or brought low for thee.
Let me be full, let me be empty.
Let me have all things, let me have nothing.
I freely and heartily yield all things
to thy pleasure and disposal.
And now, O glorious and blessed God,
Father, Son, and Holy Spirit,
thou art mine, and I am thine. So be it.
And the covenant which I have made on earth,
let it be ratified in heaven. **Amen.**

Prayers and Blessings

A Service for Upholding a Resident Moving From Independent Living to Nursing Care

LEADER: We come together to ask God's blessing on ________________ as he/she makes this move to Room ____________.

We know all of life has its transitions and turning points. What God said through Joshua to the Israelites is the word he/she needs to hear today.

"Have I not commanded you? Be strong and of good courage; do not be afraid, nor be dismayed, for the Lord your God is with you wherever you go" (Joshua 1:9, *New King James Version*).

Gracious God, whose loving hand has been on us throughout life and whose presence is ever with us; we pray at this moment for ________________. Give him/her confidence in your care and ceaseless love as he/she moves into another phase of life.

OTHERS: Nothing can separate us from the love of God.

LEADER: In the name of Jesus Christ we pray for those who serve residents in this place; grant them compassion and staying power.

OTHERS: Hear our prayer, O God.

LEADER: Give courage, O God, to ________ your servant in his/her new room. Help him/her to know the support of friends and your care. Let him/her know that you will never forsake him/her.

OTHERS: **Hear our prayer, O God, and give us your peace. Amen.**

A Room Blessing for a New Resident

RESIDENT/LEADER: We are here to welcome a new friend, ____________, into ______________ and to ask God's blessing upon this room prepared for her/his use. We know that "unless the Lord build the house, they labor in vain that build it," and no place can be home without God's presence.

ADMINISTRATOR/MINISTER: We are here to reassure you that God is present with you as you live in this room. God is your refuge and strength...your ever present help. We remember how the psalmist found that a sparrow found a home at the altar of God. So, we know you will find a home in this room and with us in this place.

LET US PRAY: (*Resident reads prayer with visitors if he/she is able to do so.*) **[Gracious God], you have set the solitary in families, and we ask now that you make your servant feel part of a family here. Your Son, Jesus, grew up as a part of a family at Nazareth. By his presence he blessed the home of Mary, Martha, and Lazarus at Bethany. Now we pray that you will make this room a place of blessing; here may it become a haven of rest, and a place of joy. "O Lord, support us all the day long, until the shadows lengthen and the evening comes, and the busy world is hushed, and the fever of life is over, and our work is done. Then in your mercy grant us a safe lodging, and a rest, and peace at last." Amen.**

A Litany for Aging

LEADER: "Then the LORD said, 'My spirit shall not abide in mortals forever, for they are flesh; their days shall be one hundred twenty years'" (Genesis 6:3).

PEOPLE: Dear Lord, we do need time to grow.

LEADER: "Honor your father and your mother, so that your days may be long in the land that the LORD your God is giving you" (Exodus 20:12).

PEOPLE: We pray that the long years will be good years.

LEADER: "The glory of youth is their strength, but the beauty of the aged is their gray hair" (Proverbs 20:29).

PEOPLE: Give us strength and experience.

LEADER: "Remember the days of old, consider the years long past; ask your father, and he will inform you; your elders, and they will tell you" (Deuteronomy 32:7).

PEOPLE: Remind us to ask, and teach us to listen.

LEADER: "Gray hair is a crown of glory; it is gained in a righteous life" (Proverbs 16:31).

PEOPLE: **Day by day we strive to be more holy.**

LEADER: "Listen to your father who begot you, and do not despise your mother when she is old" (Proverbs 23:22).

PEOPLE: **We are grateful for parents who teach and nurture in love.**

LEADER: "So even to old age and gray hairs, O God, do not forsake me, until I proclaim your might to all the generations to come" (Psalm 71:18).

PEOPLE: **We love to tell the story of Jesus and his love.**

LEADER: "In old age they still produce fruit; they are always green and full of sap" (Psalm 92:14).

PEOPLE: **We must look past the wrinkles and see the soul.**

LEADER: "You who are younger must accept the authority of the elders" (1 Peter 5:5).

PEOPLE: **Yes, we too will soon know and understand. Give us wisdom so that we may serve others as we have been served. Amen.**

A Mighty Fortress Is Our God

1. A mighty fortress is our God,
   a bulwark never failing;
   our helper he amid the flood
   of mortal ills prevailing.
   For still our ancient foe
   doth seek to work us woe;
   his craft and power are great,
   and armed with cruel hate,
   on earth is not his equal.

2. Did we in our own strength confide,
   our striving would be losing,
   were not the right man on our side,
   the man of God's own choosing.
   Dost ask who that may be?
   Christ Jesus, it is he;
   Lord Sabaoth, his name,
   from age to age the same,
   and he must win the battle.

3. That word above all earthly powers,
   no thanks to them, abideth;
   the Spirit and the gifts are ours,
   thru him who with us sideth.
   Let goods and kindred go,
   this mortal life also;
   the body they may kill;
   God's truth abideth still;
   his kingdom is forever.

Abide With Me

1. Abide with me; fast falls the eventide;
   the darkness deepens; Lord, with me abide.
   When other helpers fail and comforts flee,
   Help of the helpless, O abide with me.

2. Swift to its close ebbs out life's little day;
   earth's joys grow dim; its glories pass away;
   change and decay in all around I see;
   O thou who changest not, abide with me.

3. I need thy presence every passing hour.
   What but thy grace can
   foil the tempter's power?
   Who, like thyself, my guide and stay can be?
   Through cloud and sunshine, Lord,
   abide with me.

4. I fear no foe, with thee at hand to bless;
   ills have no weight, and tears no bitterness.
   Where is death's sting? Where,
   grave, thy victory?
   I triumph still, if thou abide with me.

5. Hold thou thy cross before my closing eyes;
   shine through the gloom
   and point me to the skies.
   Heaven's morning breaks,
   and earth's vain shadows flee;
   in life, in death, O Lord, abide with me.

Alas! and Did My Savior Bleed

1. Alas! and did my Savior bleed,
 and did my Sovereign die?
 Would he devote that sacred head
 for sinners such as I?
 At the cross, at the cross,
 where I first saw the light,
 and the burden of my heart rolled away;
 it was there by faith I received my sight,
 and now I am happy all the day.

2. Well might the sun in darkness hide,
 and shut its glories in,
 when God, the mighty maker, died
 for his own creature's sin.
 At the cross, at the cross,
 where I first saw the light,
 and the burden of my heart rolled away;
 it was there by faith I received my sight,
 and now I am happy all the day.

3. But drops of tears can ne'er repay
 the debt of love I owe.
 Here, Lord, I give myself away;
 'tis all that I can do.
 At the cross, at the cross,
 where I first saw the light,
 and the burden of my heart rolled away;
 it was there by faith I received my sight,
 and now I am happy all the day.

All Creatures of Our God and King

1. All creatures of our God and King,
   lift up your voice and with us sing,
   O praise ye! Alleluia!
   O brother sun with golden beam,
   O sister moon with silver gleam!
   O praise ye! O praise ye!
   Alleluia! Alleluia! Alleluia!

2. All ye who are of tender heart,
   forgiving others, take your part,
   O praise ye! Alleluia!
   Ye who long pain and sorrow bear,
   praise God and on him cast your care!
   O praise ye! O praise ye!
   Alleluia! Alleluia! Alleluia!

3. Let all things their Creator bless,
   and worship him in humbleness,
   O praise ye! Alleluia!
   Praise, praise the Father, praise the Son,
   and praise the Spirit, Three in One!
   O praise ye! O praise ye!
   Alleluia! Alleluia! Alleluia!

All Glory, Laud, and Honor

1. All glory, laud, and honor,
   to thee, Redeemer, King,
   to whom the lips of children
   made sweet hosannas ring.
   Thou art the King of Israel,
   thou David's royal Son,
   who in the Lord's name comest,
   the King and Blessed One.

2. All glory, laud, and honor,
   to thee, Redeemer, King,
   to whom the lips of children
   made sweet hosannas ring.
   The company of angels
   are praising thee on high,
   and we with all creation
   in chorus make reply.

3. All glory, laud, and honor,
   to thee, Redeemer, King,
   to whom the lips of children
   made sweet hosannas ring.
   Thou didst accept their praises;
   accept the prayers we bring,
   who in all good delightest,
   thou good and gracious King.

All Hail the Power of Jesus' Name

1. All hail the power of Jesus' name!
   Let angels prostrate fall;
   bring forth the royal diadem,
   and crown him Lord of all.
   Bring forth the royal diadem,
   and crown him Lord of all.

2. Ye chosen seed of Israel's race,
   ye ransomed from the fall,
   hail him who saves you by his grace,
   and crown him Lord of all.
   Hail him who saves you by his grace,
   and crown him Lord of all.

3. Let every kindred, every tribe
   on this terrestrial ball,
   to him all majesty ascribe,
   and crown him Lord of all.
   To him all majesty ascribe,
   and crown him Lord of all.

4. O that with yonder sacred throng
   we at his feet may fall!
   We'll join the everlasting song,
   and crown him Lord of all.
   We'll join the everlasting song,
   and crown him Lord of all.

Amazing Grace

1. Amazing grace! How sweet the sound
   that saved a wretch like me!
   I once was lost, but now am found;
   was blind, but now I see.

2. ’Twas grace that taught my heart to fear,
   and grace my fears relieved;
   how precious did that grace appear
   the hour I first believed.

3. Through many dangers, toils, and snares,
   I have already come;
   ’tis grace hath brought me safe thus far,
   and grace will lead me home.

4. The Lord has promised good to me,
   his word my hope secures;
   he will my shield and portion be,
   as long as life endures.

5. Yea, when this flesh and heart shall fail,
   and mortal life shall cease,
   I shall possess, within the veil,
   a life of joy and peace.

6. When we’ve been there ten thousand years,
   bright shining as the sun,
   we’ve no less days to sing God’s praise
   than when we’d first begun.

America

1. My country, 'tis of thee,
   sweet land of liberty, of thee I sing;
   land where my fathers died,
   land of the pilgrims' pride,
   from every mountainside
   let freedom ring!

2. My native country, thee,
   land of the noble free, thy name I love;
   I love thy rocks and rills,
   thy woods and templed hills;
   my heart with rapture thrills,
   like that above.

3. Let music swell the breeze,
   and ring from all the trees
   sweet freedom's song;
   let mortal tongues awake;
   let all that breathe partake;
   let rocks their silence break,
   the sound prolong.

4. Our fathers' God, to thee,
   author of liberty, to thee we sing;
   long may our land be bright
   with freedom's holy light;
   protect us by thy might,
   great God, our King.

America the Beautiful

1. O beautiful for spacious skies,
   for amber waves of grain;
   for purple mountain majesties
   above the fruited plain!
   America! America!
   God shed his grace on thee,
   and crown thy good with brotherhood
   from sea to shining sea.

2. O beautiful for heroes proved
   in liberating strife,
   who more than self their country loved,
   and mercy more than life!
   America! America!
   May God thy gold refine,
   till all success be nobleness,
   and every gain divine.

3. O beautiful for patriot dream
   that sees beyond the years
   thine alabaster cities gleam,
   undimmed by human tears!
   America! America!
   God mend thine every flaw,
   confirm thy soul in self-control,
   thy liberty in law.

Angels We Have Heard on High

1. Angels we have heard on high
   sweetly singing o'er the plains,
   and the mountains in reply
   echoing their joyous strains.
   Gloria, in excelsis Deo!
   Gloria, in excelsis Deo!

2. Shepherds, why this jubilee?
   Why your joyous strains prolong?
   What the gladsome tidings be
   which inspire your heavenly song?
   Gloria, in excelsis Deo!
   Gloria, in excelsis Deo!

3. Come to Bethlehem and see
   Christ whose birth the angels sing;
   come, adore on bended knee,
   Christ the Lord, the newborn King.
   Gloria, in excelsis Deo!
   Gloria, in excelsis Deo!

4. See him in a manger laid,
   whom the choirs of angels praise;
   Mary, Joseph, lend your aid,
   while our hearts in love we raise.
   Gloria, in excelsis Deo!
   Gloria, in excelsis Deo!

Away in a Manger

1. Away in a manger, no crib for a bed,
   the little Lord Jesus laid down his sweet head.
   The stars in the sky looked down where he lay,
   the little Lord Jesus, asleep on the hay.

2. The cattle are lowing, the baby awakes,
   but little Lord Jesus, no crying he makes;
   I love thee, Lord Jesus, look down from the sky
   and stay by my cradle till morning is nigh.

3. Be near me, Lord Jesus, I ask thee to stay
   close by me forever, and love me, I pray;
   bless all the dear children in thy tender care,
   and fit us for heaven to live with thee there.

Beneath the Cross of Jesus

1. Beneath the cross of Jesus
   I fain would take my stand,
   the shadow of a mighty rock
   within a weary land;
   a home within the wilderness,
   a rest upon the way,
   from the burning of the noontide heat,
   and the burden of the day.

2. Upon that cross of Jesus
   mine eye at times can see
   the very dying form of One
   who suffered there for me;
   and from my stricken heart with tears
   two wonders I confess:
   the wonders of redeeming love
   and my unworthiness.

3. I take, O cross, thy shadow
   for my abiding place;
   I ask no other sunshine than
   the sunshine of his face;
   content to let the world go by,
   to know no gain nor loss,
   my sinful self my only shame,
   my glory all the cross.

Blessed Assurance

1. Blessed assurance, Jesus is mine!
   O what a foretaste of glory divine!
   Heir of salvation, purchase of God,
   born of his Spirit, washed in his blood.
   This is my story, this is my song,
   praising my Savior all the day long;
   this is my story, this is my song,
   praising my Savior all the day long.

2. Perfect submission, perfect delight,
   visions of rapture now burst on my sight;
   angels descending bring from above
   echoes of mercy, whispers of love.
   This is my story, this is my song,
   praising my Savior all the day long;
   this is my story, this is my song,
   praising my Savior all the day long.

3. Perfect submission, all is at rest;
   I in my Savior am happy and blest,
   watching and waiting, looking above,
   filled with his goodness, lost in his love.
   This is my story, this is my song,
   praising my Savior all the day long;
   this is my story, this is my song,
   praising my Savior all the day long.

Breathe on Me, Breath of God

1. Breathe on me, Breath of God,
   fill me with life anew,
   that I may love what thou dost love,
   and do what thou wouldst do.

2. Breathe on me, Breath of God,
   until my heart is pure,
   until with thee I will one will,
   to do and to endure.

3. Breathe on me, Breath of God,
   till I am wholly thine,
   till all this earthly part of me
   glows with thy fire divine.

4. Breathe on me, Breath of God,
   so shall I never die,
   but live with thee the perfect life
   of thine eternity.

Christ the Lord Is Risen Today

1. Christ the Lord is risen today, Alleluia!
   Earth and heaven in chorus say, Alleluia!
   Raise your joys and triumphs high, Alleluia!
   Sing, ye heavens, and earth reply, Alleluia!

2. Love's redeeming work is done, Alleluia!
   Fought the fight, the battle won, Alleluia!
   Death in vain forbids him rise, Alleluia!
   Christ has opened paradise, Alleluia!

3. Lives again our glorious King, Alleluia!
   Where, O death, is now thy sting? Alleluia!
   Once he died our souls to save, Alleluia!
   Where's thy victory, boasting grave? Alleluia!

4. Soar we now where Christ has led, Alleluia!
   Following our exalted Head, Alleluia!
   Made like him, like him we rise, Alleluia!
   Ours the cross, the grave, the skies, Alleluia!

5. Hail the Lord of earth and heaven, Alleluia!
   Praise to thee by both be given, Alleluia!
   Thee we greet triumphant now, Alleluia!
   Hail the Resurrection, thou, Alleluia!

6. King of glory, soul of bliss, Alleluia!
   Everlasting life is this, Alleluia!
   Thee to know, thy power to prove, Alleluia!
   Thus to sing, and thus to love, Alleluia!

Come, Thou Almighty King

1. Come, thou almighty King,
   help us thy name to sing,
   help us to praise!
   Father all glorious,
   o'er all victorious,
   come and reign over us, Ancient of Days!

2. Come, thou incarnate Word,
   gird on thy mighty sword,
   our prayer attend!
   Come, and thy people bless,
   and give thy word success;
   Spirit of holiness, on us descend!

3. Come, holy Comforter,
   thy sacred witness bear
   in this glad hour.
   Thou who almighty art,
   now rule in every heart,
   and ne'er from us depart, Spirit of power!

4. To thee, great One in Three,
   eternal praises be,
   hence, evermore.
   Thy sovereign majesty
   may we in glory see,
   and to eternity love and adore!

Come, Thou Long-Expected Jesus

1. Come, thou long-expected Jesus,
   born to set thy people free;
   from our fears and sins release us,
   let us find our rest in thee.
   Israel's strength and consolation,
   hope of all the earth thou art;
   dear desire of every nation,
   joy of every longing heart.

2. Born thy people to deliver,
   born a child and yet a King,
   born to reign in us forever,
   now thy gracious kingdom bring.
   By thine own eternal spirit
   rule in all our hearts alone;
   by thine all sufficient merit,
   raise us to thy glorious throne.

Crown Him With Many Crowns

1. Crown him with many crowns,
   the Lamb upon his throne.
   Hark! how the heavenly anthem drowns
   all music but its own.
   Awake, my soul, and sing
   of him who died for thee,
   and hail him as thy matchless King
   through all eternity.

2. Crown him the Lord of life,
   who triumphed o'er the grave,
   and rose victorious in the strife
   for those he came to save.
   His glories now we sing,
   who died, and rose on high,
   who died, eternal life to bring,
   and lives that death may die.

3. Crown him the Lord of love;
   behold his hands and side,
   those wounds, yet visible above,
   in beauty glorified.
   All hail, Redeemer, hail!
   For thou hast died for me;
   thy praise and glory shall not fail
   throughout eternity.

Fairest Lord Jesus

1. Fairest Lord Jesus, ruler of all nature,
   O thou of God and man the Son,
   thee will I cherish, thee will I honor,
   thou, my soul's glory, joy, and crown.

2. Fair are the meadows,
   fairer still the woodlands,
   robed in the blooming garb of spring:
   Jesus is fairer, Jesus is purer,
   who makes the woeful heart to sing.

3. Fair is the sunshine, fairer still the moonlight,
   and all the twinkling starry host:
   Jesus shines brighter, Jesus shines purer
   than all the angels heaven can boast.

4. Beautiful Savior! Lord of all the nations!
   Son of God and Son of Man!
   Glory and honor, praise, adoration,
   now and forevermore be thine.

Faith of Our Fathers

1. Faith of our fathers, living still,
   in spite of dungeon, fire, and sword;
   O how our hearts beat high with joy
   whene'er we hear that glorious word!
   Faith of our fathers, holy faith!
   We will be true to thee till death.

2. Faith of our fathers, we will strive
   to win all nations unto thee;
   and through the truth that comes from God,
   we all shall then be truly free.
   Faith of our fathers, holy faith!
   We will be true to thee till death.

3. Faith of our fathers, we will love
   both friend and foe in all our strife;
   and preach thee, too, as love knows how
   by kindly words and virtuous life.
   Faith of our fathers, holy faith!
   We will be true to thee till death.

For the Beauty of the Earth

1. For the beauty of the earth,
   for the glory of the skies,
   for the love which from our birth
   over and around us lies;
   Lord of all, to thee we raise
   this our hymn of grateful praise.

2. For the beauty of each hour
   of the day and of the night,
   hill and vale, and tree and flower,
   sun and moon, and stars of light;
   Lord of all, to thee we raise
   this our hymn of grateful praise.

3. For the joy of human love,
   brother, sister, parent, child,
   friends on earth and friends above,
   for all gentle thoughts and mild;
   Lord of all, to thee we raise
   this our hymn of grateful praise.

4. For thyself, best Gift Divine,
   to the world so freely given,
   for that great, great love of thine,
   peace on earth, and joy in heaven:
   Lord of all, to thee we raise
   this our hymn of grateful praise.

Go, Tell It on the Mountain

1. Go, tell it on the mountain,
over the hills and everywhere;
go, tell it on the mountain,
that Jesus Christ is born.
While shepherds kept their watching
o'er silent flocks by night,
behold throughout the heavens
there shone a holy light.

2. Go, tell it on the mountain,
over the hills and everywhere;
go, tell it on the mountain,
that Jesus Christ is born.
The shepherds feared and trembled,
when lo! above the earth,
rang out the angel chorus
that hailed the Savior's birth.

3. Go, tell it on the mountain,
over the hills and everywhere;
go, tell it on the mountain,
that Jesus Christ is born.
Down in a lowly manger
the humble Christ was born,
and God sent us salvation
that blessed Christmas morn.

God Be With You Till We Meet Again

1. God be with you till we meet again;
   by his counsels guide, uphold you,
   with his sheep securely fold you;

   Refrain
   God be with you till we meet again.
   Till we meet, till we meet,
   till we meet at Jesus' feet;
   till we meet, till we meet,
   God be with you till we meet again.

2. God be with you till we meet again;
   neath his wings securely hide you,
   daily manna still provide you;
   Refrain

3. God be with you till we meet again;
   when life's perils thick confound you,
   put his arms unfailing round you;
   Refrain

4. God be with you till we meet again;
   keep love's banner floating o'er you,
   smite death's threatening wave before you;
   Refrain

Hail to the Lord's Anointed

1. Hail to the Lord's Anointed,
   great David's greater Son!
   Hail in the time appointed,
   his reign on earth begun!
   He comes to break oppression,
   to set the captive free;
   to take away transgression,
   and rule in equity.

2. He comes with succor speedy
   to those who suffer wrong;
   to help the poor and needy,
   and bid the weak be strong;
   to give them songs for sighing,
   their darkness turn to light,
   whose souls, condemned and dying,
   are precious in his sight.

3. To him shall prayer unceasing
   and daily vows ascend;
   his kingdom still increasing,
   a kingdom without end.
   The tide of time shall never
   his covenant remove;
   his name shall stand forever;
   that name to us is love.

Hark! The Herald Angels Sing

1. Hark! the herald angels sing,
   "Glory to the newborn King;
   peace on earth, and mercy mild,
   God and sinners reconciled!"
   Joyful, all ye nations rise,
   join the triumph of the skies;
   with th'angelic host proclaim,
   "Christ is born in Bethlehem!"
   Hark! the herald angels sing,
   "Glory to the newborn King!"

2. Hail the heaven-born Prince of Peace!
   Hail the Sun of Righteousness!
   Light and life to all he brings,
   risen with healing in his wings.
   Mild he lays his glory by,
   born that we no more may die,
   born to raise us from the earth,
   born to give us second birth.
   Hark! the herald angels sing,
   "Glory to the newborn King!"

Have Thine Own Way, Lord

1. Have thine own way, Lord!
   Have thine own way!
   Thou art the potter; I am the clay.
   Mold me and make me after thy will,
   while I am waiting, yielded and still.

2. Have thine own way, Lord!
   Have thine own way!
   Search me and try me, Savior today!
   Wash me just now, Lord, wash me just now,
   as in thy presence humbly I bow.

3. Have thine own way, Lord!
   Have thine own way!
   Wounded and weary, help me I pray!
   Power, all power, surely is thine!
   Touch me and heal me, Savior divine!

4. Have thine own way, Lord!
   Have thine own way!
   Hold o'er my being absolute sway.
   Fill with thy Spirit till all shall see
   Christ only, always, living in me!

He Leadeth Me: O Blessed Thought

1. He leadeth me: O blessed thought!
   O words with heavenly comfort fraught!
   Whate'er I do, where'er I be,
   still 'tis God's hand that leadeth me.

   Refrain
   He leadeth me, he leadeth me,
   by his own hand he leadeth me;
   his faithful follower I would be,
   for by his hand he leadeth me.

2. Sometimes mid scenes of deepest gloom,
   sometimes where Eden's bowers bloom,
   by waters still, o'er troubled sea,
   still 'tis his hand that leadeth me.
   Refrain

3. Lord, I would place my hand in thine,
   nor ever murmur nor repine;
   content, whatever lot I see,
   since 'tis my God that leadeth me.
   Refrain

4. And when my task on earth is done,
   when by thy grace the victory's won,
   e'en death's cold wave I will not flee,
   since God through Jordan leadeth me.
   Refrain

He Lives

1. I serve a risen Savior, he's in the world today;
   I know that he is living, whatever foes may say.
   I see his hand of mercy, I hear his voice of cheer,
   and just the time I need him, he's always near.
   Refrain
   He lives (he lives), he lives (he lives),
   Christ Jesus lives today!
   He walks with me and talks with me
   along life's narrow way.
   He lives (he lives), he lives (he lives),
   salvation to impart!
   You ask me how I know he lives?
   He lives within my heart.

2. In all the world around me I see his loving care,
   and though my heart grows weary,
   I never will despair.
   I know that he is leading
   through all the stormy blast;
   the day of his appearing will come at last.
   Refrain

3. Rejoice, rejoice, O Christian,
   lift up your voice and sing
   eternal hallelujahs to Jesus Christ the King!
   The hope of all who seek him,
   the help of all who find;
   none other is so loving, so good and kind.
   Refrain

Holy, Holy, Holy! Lord God Almighty

1. Holy, holy, holy! Lord God Almighty!
   Early in the morning
   our song shall rise to thee.
   Holy, holy, holy! Merciful and mighty,
   God in three persons, blessed Trinity!

2. Holy, holy, holy! All the saints adore thee,
   casting down their golden crowns
   around the glassy sea;
   cherubim and seraphim
   falling down before thee,
   which wert, and art, and evermore shalt be.

3. Holy, holy, holy!
   Though the darkness hide thee,
   though the eye of sinful man
   thy glory may not see,
   only thou art holy; there is none beside thee,
   perfect in power, in love and purity.

4. Holy, holy, holy! Lord God Almighty!
   All thy works shall praise thy name,
   in earth and sky and sea.
   Holy, holy, holy! Merciful and mighty,
   God in three persons, blessed Trinity.

How Firm a Foundation

1. How firm a foundation, ye saints of the Lord,
is laid for your faith in his excellent word!
What more can he say
than to you he hath said,
to you who for refuge to Jesus have fled?

2. "Fear not, I am with thee, O be not dismayed,
for I am thy God and will still give thee aid;
I'll strengthen and help thee,
and cause thee to stand
upheld by my righteous, omnipotent hand.

3. "When through the deep waters
I call thee to go,
the rivers of woe shall not thee overflow;
for I will be with thee, thy troubles to bless,
and sanctify to thee thy deepest distress.

4. "When through fiery trials
thy pathways shall lie,
my grace, all-sufficient, shall be thy supply;
the flame shall not hurt thee; I only design
thy dross to consume, and thy gold to refine.

5. "The soul that on Jesus still leans for repose,
I will not, I will not desert to its foes;
that soul, though all hell
should endeavor to shake,
I'll never, no, never, no, never forsake."

I Am Thine, O Lord

1. I am thine, O Lord, I have heard thy voice,
   and it told thy love to me;
   but I long to rise in the arms of faith
   and be closer drawn to thee.

   Refrain
   Draw me nearer, nearer, blessed Lord,
   to the cross where thou hast died.
   Draw me nearer, nearer, nearer, blessed Lord,
   to thy precious, bleeding side.

2. Consecrate me now to thy service, Lord,
   by the power of grace divine;
   let my soul look up with a steadfast hope,
   and my will be lost in thine.
   Refrain

3. O the pure delight of a single hour
   that before thy throne I spend,
   when I kneel in prayer,
   and with thee, my God,
   I commune as friend with friend!
   Refrain

4. There are depths of love that I cannot know
   till I cross the narrow sea;
   there are heights of joy that I may not reach
   till I rest in peace with thee.
   Refrain

I Love to Tell the Story

1. I love to tell the story of unseen things above,
   of Jesus and his glory, of Jesus and his love.
   I love to tell the story, because I know ’tis true;
   it satisfies my longings as nothing else can do.

   Refrain
   I love to tell the story,
   ’twill be my theme in glory,
   to tell the old, old story of Jesus and his love.

2. I love to tell the story; ’tis pleasant to repeat
   what seems, each time I tell it,
   more wonderfully sweet.
   I love to tell the story,
   for some have never heard
   the message of salvation
   from God’s own holy Word.
   Refrain

3. I love to tell the story,
   for those who know it best
   seem hungering and thirsting
   to hear it like the rest.
   And when, in scenes of glory,
   I sing the new, new song,
   ’twill be the old, old story
   that I have loved so long.
   Refrain

I Need Thee Every Hour

1. I need thee every hour, most gracious Lord;
   no tender voice like thine can peace afford.

   Refrain
   I need thee, O I need thee;
   every hour I need thee;
   O bless me now, my Savior, I come to thee.

2. I need thee every hour; stay thou nearby;
   temptations lose their power
   when thou art nigh.
   Refrain

3. I need thee every hour, in joy or pain;
   come quickly and abide, or life is vain.
   Refrain

4. I need thee every hour; teach me thy will;
   and thy rich promises in me fulfill.
   Refrain

5. I need thee every hour, most Holy One;
   O make me thine indeed, thou blessed Son.
   Refrain

In the Garden

1. I come to the garden alone
while the dew is still on the roses,
and the voice I hear falling on my ear,
the Son of God discloses.
And he walks with me, and he talks with me,
and he tells me I am his own;
and the joy we share as we tarry there,
none other has ever known.

2. He speaks, and the sound of his voice
is so sweet the birds hush their singing,
and the melody that he gave to me
within my heart is ringing.
And he walks with me, and he talks with me,
and he tells me I am his own;
and the joy we share as we tarry there,
none other has ever known.

3. I'd stay in the garden with him
though the night around me be falling,
but he bids me go; thru the voice of woe
his voice to me is calling.
And he walks with me, and he talks with me,
and he tells me I am his own;
and the joy we share as we tarry there,
none other has ever known.

It Came Upon the Midnight Clear

1. It came upon the midnight clear,
that glorious song of old,
from angels bending near the earth,
to touch their harps of gold:
"Peace on the earth, good will to men,
from heaven's all-gracious King."
The world in solemn stillness lay,
to hear the angels sing.

2. Still through the cloven skies they come
with peaceful wings unfurled,
and still their heavenly music floats
o'er all the weary world;
above its sad and lowly plains,
they bend on hovering wing,
and ever o'er its Babel sounds
the blessed angels sing.

3. For lo! the days are hastening on,
by prophet seen of old,
when with the ever-circling years
shall come the time foretold
when peace shall over all the earth
its ancient splendors fling,
and the whole world send back the song
which now the angels sing.

It Is Well With My Soul

1. When peace, like a river, attendeth my way,
   when sorrows like sea billows roll;
   whatever my lot, thou hast taught me to say,
   It is well, it is well with my soul.

   Refrain
   It is well with my soul,
   it is well, it is well with my soul.

2. Though Satan should buffet,
   though trials should come,
   let this blest assurance control,
   that Christ has regarded my helpless estate,
   and hath shed his own blood for my soul.
   Refrain

3. My sin, oh, the bliss of this glorious thought!
   My sin, not in part but the whole,
   is nailed to the cross, and I bear it no more,
   praise the Lord, praise the Lord, O my soul!
   Refrain

4. And, Lord, haste the day
   when my faith shall be sight,
   the clouds be rolled back as a scroll;
   the trump shall resound,
   and the Lord shall descend,
   even so, it is well with my soul.
   Refrain

Jesus, Keep Me Near the Cross

1. Jesus, keep me near the cross;
   there a precious fountain,
   free to all, a healing stream,
   flows from Calvary's mountain.

   Refrain
   In the cross, in the cross,
   be my glory ever,
   till my raptured soul shall find
   rest beyond the river.

2. Near the cross, a trembling soul,
   love and mercy found me;
   there the bright and morning star
   sheds its beams around me.
   Refrain

3. Near the cross! O Lamb of God,
   bring its scenes before me;
   help me walk from day to day
   with its shadow o'er me.
   Refrain

4. Near the cross I'll watch and wait,
   hoping, trusting ever,
   till I reach the golden strand
   just beyond the river.
   Refrain

Jesus Loves Me

1. Jesus loves me! This I know,
   for the Bible tells me so.
   Little ones to him belong;
   they are weak, but he is strong.
   Yes, Jesus loves me!
   Yes, Jesus loves me!
   Yes, Jesus loves me!
   The Bible tells me so.

2. Jesus loves me! This I know,
   as he loved so long ago,
   taking children on his knee,
   saying, "Let them come to me."
   Yes, Jesus loves me!
   Yes, Jesus loves me!
   Yes, Jesus loves me!
   The Bible tells me so.

3. Jesus loves me still today,
   walking with me on my way,
   wanting as a friend to give
   light and love to all who live.
   Yes, Jesus loves me!
   Yes, Jesus loves me!
   Yes, Jesus loves me!
   The Bible tells me so.

Joy to the World

1. Joy to the world, the Lord is come!
   Let earth receive her King;
   let every heart prepare him room,
   and heaven and nature sing,
   and heaven and nature sing,
   and heaven, and heaven, and nature sing.

2. Joy to the world, the Savior reigns!
   Let all their songs employ;
   while fields and floods, rocks, hills, and plains
   repeat the sounding joy,
   repeat the sounding joy,
   repeat, repeat the sounding joy.

3. No more let sins and sorrows grow,
   nor thorns infest the ground;
   he comes to make his blessings flow
   far as the curse is found,
   far as the curse is found,
   far as, far as the curse is found.

4. He rules the world with truth and grace,
   and makes the nations prove
   the glories of his righteousness,
   and wonders of his love,
   and wonders of his love,
   and wonders, wonders of his love.

Joyful, Joyful, We Adore Thee

1. Joyful, joyful, we adore thee,
   God of glory, Lord of love;
   hearts unfold like flowers before thee,
   opening to the sun above.
   Melt the clouds of sin and sadness;
   drive the dark of doubt away.
   Giver of immortal gladness,
   fill us with the light of day!

2. All thy works with joy surround thee,
   earth and heaven reflect thy rays,
   stars and angels sing around thee,
   center of unbroken praise.
   Field and forest, vale and mountain,
   flowery meadow, flashing sea,
   chanting bird and flowing fountain,
   call us to rejoice in thee.

3. Mortals, join the mighty chorus
   which the morning stars began;
   love divine is reigning o'er us,
   binding all within its span.
   Ever singing, march we onward,
   victors in the midst of strife;
   joyful music leads us sunward,
   in the triumph song of life.

Just As I Am, Without One Plea

1. Just as I am, without one plea,
   but that thy blood was shed for me,
   and that thou bidst me come to thee,
   O Lamb of God, I come, I come.

2. Just as I am, and waiting not
   to rid my soul of one dark blot,
   to thee whose blood can cleanse each spot,
   O Lamb of God, I come, I come.

3. Just as I am, though tossed about
   with many a conflict, many a doubt,
   fightings and fears within, without,
   O Lamb of God, I come, I come.

4. Just as I am, poor, wretched, blind;
   sight, riches, healing of the mind,
   yea, all I need in thee to find,
   O Lamb of God, I come, I come.

5. Just as I am, thou wilt receive,
   wilt welcome, pardon, cleanse, relieve;
   because thy promise I believe,
   O Lamb of God, I come, I come.

6. Just as I am, thy love unknown
   hath broken every barrier down;
   now, to be thine, yea, thine alone,
   O Lamb of God, I come, I come.

Leaning on the Everlasting Arms

1. What a fellowship, what a joy divine,
leaning on the everlasting arms;
what a blessedness, what a peace is mine,
leaning on the everlasting arms.

Refrain
Leaning, leaning,
safe and secure from all alarms;
leaning, leaning,
leaning on the everlasting arms.

2. O how sweet to walk in this pilgrim way,
leaning on the everlasting arms;
O how bright the path grows from day to day,
leaning on the everlasting arms.
Refrain

3. What have I to dread, what have I to fear,
leaning on the everlasting arms?
I have blessed peace with my Lord so near,
leaning on the everlasting arms.
Refrain

Let Us Break Bread Together

1. Let us break bread together on our knees,
   let us break bread together on our knees.
   When I fall on my knees
   with my face to the rising sun,
   O Lord, have mercy on me.

2. Let us drink wine together on our knees,
   let us drink wine together on our knees.
   When I fall on my knees
   with my face to the rising sun,
   O Lord, have mercy on me.

3. Let us praise God together on our knees,
   let us praise God together on our knees.
   When I fall on my knees
   with my face to the rising sun,
   O Lord, have mercy on me.

4. Let us praise God together on our knees,
   let us praise God together on our knees.
   When I fall on my knees
   with my face to the rising sun,
   O Lord, have mercy if you please.

Lift Every Voice and Sing

1. Lift every voice and sing,
   till earth and heaven ring,
   ring with the harmonies of liberty;
   let our rejoicing rise
   high as the listening skies,
   let it resound loud as the rolling sea.
   Sing a song full of the faith
   that the dark past has taught us;
   sing a song full of the hope
   that the present has brought us;
   facing the rising sun
   of our new day begun,
   let us march on till victory is won.

2. God of our weary years,
   God of our silent tears,
   thou who hast brought us thus far on the way;
   thou who hast by thy might
   led us into the light,
   keep us forever in the path, we pray.
   Lest our feet stray from the places,
   our God, where we met thee;
   lest our hearts drunk with the
   wine of the world, we forget thee;
   shadowed beneath thy hand,
   may we forever stand,
   true to our God, true to our native land.

Lift Up Your Heads, Ye Mighty Gates

1. Lift up your heads, ye mighty gates;
   behold, the King of glory waits;
   the King of kings is drawing near;
   the Savior of the world is here!

2. Fling wide the portals of your heart;
   make it a temple, set apart
   from earthly use for heaven's employ,
   adorned with prayer and love and joy.

3. Redeemer, come, with us abide;
   our hearts to thee we open wide;
   let us thy inner presence feel;
   thy grace and love in us reveal.

4. Thy Holy Spirit lead us on
   until our glorious goal is won;
   eternal praise, eternal fame
   be offered, Savior, to thy name!

Love Divine, All Loves Excelling

1. Love divine, all loves excelling,
   joy of heaven, to earth come down;
   fix in us thy humble dwelling;
   all thy faithful mercies crown!
   Jesus, thou art all compassion,
   pure, unbounded love thou art;
   visit us with thy salvation;
   enter every trembling heart.

2. Breathe, O breathe thy loving Spirit
   into every troubled breast!
   Let us all in thee inherit;
   let us find that second rest.
   Take away our bent to sinning;
   Alpha and Omega be;
   end of faith, as its beginning,
   set our hearts at liberty.

3. Finish, then, thy new creation;
   pure and spotless let us be.
   Let us see thy great salvation
   perfectly restored in thee;
   changed from glory into glory,
   till in heaven we take our place,
   till we cast our crowns before thee,
   lost in wonder, love, and praise.

Marching to Zion

1. Come, we that love the Lord,
   and let our joys be known;
   join in a song with sweet accord,
   join in a song with sweet accord
   and thus surround the throne,
   and thus surround the throne.

   Refrain
   We're marching to Zion,
   beautiful, beautiful Zion;
   we're marching upward to Zion,
   the beautiful city of God.

2. Let those refuse to sing
   who never knew our God;
   but children of the heavenly King,
   but children of the heavenly King
   may speak their joys abroad,
   may speak their joys abroad.
   Refrain

3. Then let our songs abound,
   and every tear be dry;
   we're marching through Emmanuel's ground,
   we're marching through Emmanuel's ground,
   to fairer worlds on high,
   to fairer worlds on high.
   Refrain

My Faith Looks Up to Thee

1. My faith looks up to thee,
   thou Lamb of Calvary,
   Savior divine!
   Now hear me while I pray,
   take all my guilt away,
   O let me from this day be wholly thine!

2. May thy rich grace impart
   strength to my fainting heart,
   my zeal inspire!
   As thou hast died for me,
   O may my love to thee
   pure, warm, and changeless be, a living fire!

3. While life's dark maze I tread,
   and griefs around me spread,
   be thou my guide;
   bid darkness turn to day,
   wipe sorrow's tears away,
   nor let me ever stray from thee aside.

4. When ends life's transient dream,
   when death's cold, sullen stream
   shall o'er me roll;
   blest Savior, then in love,
   fear and distrust remove;
   O bear me safe above, a ransomed soul!

My Hope Is Built

1. My hope is built on nothing less
than Jesus' blood and righteousness.
I dare not trust the sweetest frame,
but wholly lean on Jesus' name.

Refrain
On Christ the solid rock I stand,
all other ground is sinking sand;
all other ground is sinking sand.

2. When darkness veils his lovely face,
I rest on his unchanging grace.
In every high and stormy gale,
my anchor holds within the veil.
Refrain

3. His oath, his covenant, his blood
support me in the whelming flood.
When all around my soul gives way,
he then is all my hope and stay.
Refrain

4. When he shall come with trumpet sound,
O may I then in him be found!
Dressed in his righteousness alone,
faultless to stand before the throne!
Refrain

Near to the Heart of God

1. There is a place of quiet rest,
near to the heart of God;
a place where sin cannot molest,
near to the heart of God.
O Jesus, blest Redeemer,
sent from the heart of God,
hold us who wait before thee
near to the heart of God.

2. There is a place of comfort sweet,
near to the heart of God;
a place where we our Savior meet,
near to the heart of God.
O Jesus, blest Redeemer,
sent from the heart of God,
hold us who wait before thee
near to the heart of God.

3. There is a place of full release,
near to the heart of God;
a place where all is joy and peace,
near to the heart of God.
O Jesus, blest Redeemer,
sent from the heart of God,
hold us who wait before thee
near to the heart of God.

Nearer, My God, to Thee

1. Nearer, my God, to thee, nearer to thee!
   E'en though it be a cross that raiseth me,
   still all my song shall be,
   nearer, my God, to thee;
   nearer, my God, to thee, nearer to thee!

2. Though like the wanderer, the sun gone down,
   darkness be over me, my rest a stone;
   yet in my dreams I'd be
   nearer, my God, to thee;
   nearer, my God, to thee, nearer to thee!

3. There let the way appear, steps unto heaven;
   all that thou sendest me, in mercy given;
   angels to beckon me
   nearer, my God, to thee;
   nearer, my God, to thee, nearer to thee!

4. Then, with my waking thoughts
   bright with thy praise,
   out of my stony griefs Bethel I'll raise;
   so by my woes to be
   nearer, my God, to thee;
   nearer, my God, to thee, nearer to thee!

5. Or if, on joyful wing cleaving the sky,
   sun, moon, and stars forgot, upward I fly,
   still all my song shall be,
   nearer, my God, to thee;
   nearer, my God, to thee, nearer to thee!

Now Thank We All Our God

1. Now thank we all our God,
   with heart and hands and voices,
   who wondrous things has done,
   in whom this world rejoices;
   who from our mothers' arms
   has blessed us on our way
   with countless gifts of love,
   and still is ours today.

2. O may this bounteous God
   through all our life be near us,
   with ever joyful hearts
   and blessed peace to cheer us;
   and keep us still in grace,
   and guide us when perplexed;
   and free us from all ills,
   in this world and the next.

3. All praise and thanks to God
   the Father now be given;
   the Son, and him who reigns
   with them in highest heaven;
   the one eternal God,
   whom earth and heaven adore;
   for thus it was, is now,
   and shall be evermore.

O Come, All Ye Faithful

1. O come, all ye faithful,
   joyful and triumphant,
   O come ye, O come ye, to Bethlehem.
   Come and behold him, born the King of angels;

   Refrain
   O come, let us adore him,
   O come, let us adore him,
   O come, let us adore him,
   Christ the Lord.

2. Sing, choirs of angels,
   sing in exultation;
   O sing, all ye citizens of heaven above!
   Glory to God, all glory in the highest;
   Refrain

3. See how the shepherds,
   summoned to his cradle,
   leaving their flocks, draw nigh to gaze;
   we too will thither bend our joyful footsteps;
   Refrain

4. Yea, Lord, we greet thee,
   born this happy morning,
   Jesus, to thee be all glory given.
   Word of the Father, now in flesh appearing:
   Refrain

O Come, O Come, Emmanuel

1. O come, O come, Emmanuel,
   and ransom captive Israel,
   that mourns in lonely exile here
   until the Son of God appear.
   Refrain
   Rejoice! Rejoice! Emmanuel
   shall come to thee, O Israel.

2. O come, thou Wisdom from on high,
   and order all things far and nigh;
   to us the path of knowledge show
   and cause us in her ways to go. ***Refrain***

3. O come, thou Root of Jesse's tree,
   an ensign of thy people be;
   before thee rulers silent fall;
   all peoples on thy mercy call. ***Refrain***

4. O come, thou Dayspring, come and cheer
   our spirits by thy justice here;
   disperse the gloomy clouds of night,
   and death's dark shadows put to flight. ***Refrain***

5. O come, Desire of nations bind
   all peoples in one heart and mind.
   From dust thou brought us forth to life;
   deliver us from earthly strife. ***Refrain***

O for a Thousand Tongues to Sing

1. O for a thousand tongues to sing
   my great Redeemer's praise,
   the glories of my God and King,
   the triumphs of his grace!

2. My gracious Master and my God,
   assist me to proclaim,
   to spread through all the earth abroad
   the honors of thy name.

3. Jesus! the name that charms our fears,
   that bids our sorrows cease;
   'tis music in the sinner's ears,
   'tis life, and health, and peace.

4. He breaks the power of canceled sin,
   he sets the prisoner free;
   his blood can make the foulest clean;
   his blood availed for me.

5. He speaks, and listening to his voice,
   new life the dead receive;
   the mournful, broken hearts rejoice,
   the humble poor believe.

6. In Christ, your head, you then shall know,
   shall feel your sins forgiven;
   anticipate your heaven below,
   and own that love is heaven.

O God, Our Help in Ages Past

1. O God, our help in ages past,
   our hope for years to come,
   our shelter from the stormy blast,
   and our eternal home!

2. Under the shadow of thy throne,
   still may we dwell secure;
   sufficient is thine arm alone,
   and our defense is sure.

3. Before the hills in order stood,
   or earth received her frame,
   from everlasting, thou art God,
   to endless years the same.

4. A thousand ages, in thy sight,
   are like an evening gone;
   short as the watch that ends the night,
   before the rising sun.

5. Time, like an ever rolling stream,
   bears all who breathe away;
   they fly forgotten, as a dream
   dies at the opening day.

6. O God, our help in ages past,
   our hope for years to come;
   be thou our guide while life shall last,
   and our eternal home.

O How I Love Jesus

1. There is a name I love to hear,
   I love to sing its worth;
   it sounds like music in my ear,
   the sweetest name on earth.
   O how I love Jesus,
   O how I love Jesus,
   O how I love Jesus,
   because he first loved me!

2. It tells me of a Savior's love,
   who died to set me free;
   it tells me of his precious blood,
   the sinner's perfect plea.
   O how I love Jesus,
   O how I love Jesus,
   O how I love Jesus,
   because he first loved me!

3. It tells of one whose loving heart
   can feel my deepest woe;
   who in each sorrow bears a part
   that none can bear below.
   O how I love Jesus,
   O how I love Jesus,
   O how I love Jesus,
   because he first loved me!

O Jesus, I Have Promised

1. O Jesus, I have promised
to serve thee to the end;
be thou forever near me,
my Master and my Friend.
I shall not fear the battle
if thou art by my side,
nor wander from the pathway
if thou wilt be my guide.

2. O let me feel thee near me!
The world is ever near;
I see the sights that dazzle,
the tempting sounds I hear;
my foes are ever near me,
around me and within;
but Jesus, draw thou nearer,
and shield my soul from sin.

3. O Jesus, thou hast promised
to all who follow thee
that where thou art in glory
there shall thy servant be.
And Jesus, I have promised
to serve thee to the end;
O give me grace to follow,
my Master and my Friend.

O Little Town of Bethlehem

1. O little town of Bethlehem,
   how still we see thee lie;
   above thy deep and dreamless sleep
   the silent stars go by.
   Yet in thy dark streets shineth
   the everlasting light;
   the hopes and fears of all the years
   are met in thee tonight.

2. For Christ is born of Mary,
   and gathered all above,
   while mortals sleep, the angels keep
   their watch of wondering love.
   O morning stars together,
   proclaim the holy birth,
   and praises sing to God the King,
   and peace to all on earth!

3. O holy Child of Bethlehem,
   descend to us, we pray;
   cast out our sin, and enter in,
   be born in us today.
   We hear the Christmas angels
   the great glad tidings tell;
   O come to us, abide with us,
   our Lord Emmanuel!

O Perfect Love

1. O perfect Love, all
   human thought transcending,
   lowly we kneel in prayer before thy throne,
   that theirs may be the
   love which knows no ending,
   whom thou forevermore dost join in one.

2. O perfect Life, be thou their full assurance
   of tender charity and steadfast faith,
   of patient hope and quiet, brave endurance,
   with childlike trust that fears
   nor pain nor death.

3. Grant them the joy which
   brightens earthly sorrow;
   grant them the peace which
   calms all earthly strife,
   and to life's day the
   glorious unknown morrow
   that dawns upon eternal love and life.

Onward, Christian Soldiers

1. Onward, Christian soldiers,
   marching as to war,
   with the cross of Jesus going on before.
   Christ, the royal Master,
   leads against the foe;
   forward into battle see his banners go!

   Refrain
   Onward, Christian soldiers,
   marching as to war,
   with the cross of Jesus going on before.

2. Crowns and thrones may perish,
   kingdoms rise and wane,
   but the church of Jesus constant will remain.
   Gates of hell can never
   gainst that church prevail;
   we have Christ's own promise,
   and that cannot fail.
   Refrain

3. Onward then, ye people,
   join our happy throng,
   blend with ours your voices
   in the triumph song.
   Glory, laud, and honor unto Christ the King,
   this through countless ages
   men and angels sing.
   Refrain

Open My Eyes, That I May See

1. Open my eyes, that I may see
glimpses of truth thou hast for me;
place in my hands the wonderful key
that shall unclasp and set me free.
Silently now I wait for thee,
ready, my God, thy will to see.
Open my eyes, illumine me, Spirit divine!

2. Open my ears, that I may hear
voices of truth thou sendest clear;
and while the wavenotes fall on my ear,
everything false will disappear.
Silently now I wait for thee,
ready, my God, thy will to see.
Open my ears, illumine me, Spirit divine!

3. Open my mouth, and let me bear
gladly the warm truth everywhere;
open my heart and let me prepare
love with thy children thus to share.
Silently now I wait for thee,
ready, my God, thy will to see.
Open my heart, illumine me, Spirit divine!

Pass Me Not, O Gentle Savior

1. Pass me not, O gentle Savior,
   hear my humble cry;
   while on others thou art calling,
   do not pass me by.

   Refrain
   Savior, Savior, hear my humble cry;
   while on others thou art calling,
   do not pass me by.

2. Let me at thy throne of mercy
   find a sweet relief,
   kneeling there in deep contrition;
   help my unbelief.
   Refrain

3. Trusting only in thy merit,
   would I seek thy face;
   heal my wounded, broken spirit,
   save me by thy grace.
   Refrain

4. Thou the spring of all my comfort,
   more than life to me,
   whom have I on earth beside thee?
   Whom in heaven but thee?
   Refrain

Praise to the Lord, the Almighty

1. Praise to the Lord,
   the Almighty, the King of creation!
   O my soul, praise him,
   for he is thy health and salvation!
   All ye who hear, now to his temple draw near;
   join me in glad adoration!

2. Praise to the Lord,
   who o'er all things so wondrously reigning
   bears thee on eagle's wings,
   e'er in his keeping maintaining.
   God's care enfolds
   all, whose true good he upholds.
   Hast thou not known his sustaining?

3. Praise to the Lord,
   who doth prosper thy work and defend thee;
   surely his goodness and mercy
   here daily attend thee.
   Ponder anew what the Almighty can do,
   who with his love doth befriend thee.

4. Praise to the Lord!
   O let all that is in me adore him!
   All that hath life and breath,
   come now with praises before him!
   Let the amen sound from his people again;
   gladly forever adore him.

Rock of Ages, Cleft for Me

1. Rock of Ages, cleft for me,
   let me hide myself in thee;
   let the water and the blood,
   from thy wounded side which flowed,
   be of sin the double cure;
   save from wrath and make me pure.

2. Not the labors of my hands
   can fulfill thy law's demands;
   could my zeal no respite know,
   could my tears forever flow,
   all for sin could not atone;
   thou must save, and thou alone.

3. Nothing in my hand I bring,
   simply to the cross I cling;
   naked, come to thee for dress;
   helpless, look to thee for grace;
   foul, I to the fountain fly;
   wash me, Savior, or I die.

4. While I draw this fleeting breath,
   when mine eyes shall close in death,
   when I soar to worlds unknown,
   see thee on thy judgment throne,
   Rock of Ages, cleft for me,
   let me hide myself in thee.

Savior, Like a Shepherd Lead Us

1. Savior, like a shepherd lead us,
   much we need thy tender care;
   in thy pleasant pastures feed us,
   for our use thy folds prepare.
   Blessed Jesus, blessed Jesus!
   Thou hast bought us, thine we are.
   Blessed Jesus, blessed Jesus!
   Thou hast bought us, thine we are.

2. We are thine, thou dost befriend us,
   be the guardian of our way;
   keep thy flock, from sin defend us,
   seek us when we go astray.
   Blessed Jesus, blessed Jesus!
   Hear, O hear us when we pray.
   Blessed Jesus, blessed Jesus!
   Hear, O hear us when we pray.

3. Early let us seek thy favor,
   early let us do thy will;
   blessed Lord and only Savior,
   with thy love our bosoms fill.
   Blessed Jesus, blessed Jesus!
   Thou hast loved us, love us still.
   Blessed Jesus, blessed Jesus!
   Thou hast loved us, love us still.

Shall We Gather at the River

1. Shall we gather at the river,
   where bright angel feet have trod,
   with its crystal tide forever
   flowing by the throne of God?

   Refrain
   Yes, we'll gather at the river,
   the beautiful, the beautiful river;
   gather with the saints at the river
   that flows by the throne of God.

2. On the margin of the river,
   washing up its silver spray,
   we will walk and worship ever,
   all the happy golden day.
   Refrain

3. Ere we reach the shining river,
   lay we every burden down;
   grace our spirits will deliver,
   and provide a robe and crown.
   Refrain

4. Soon we'll reach the shining river,
   soon our pilgrimage will cease;
   soon our happy hearts will quiver
   with the melody of peace.
   Refrain

Silent Night, Holy Night

1. Silent night, holy night,
   all is calm, all is bright
   round yon virgin mother and child.
   Holy infant, so tender and mild,
   sleep in heavenly peace,
   sleep in heavenly peace.

2. Silent night, holy night,
   shepherds quake at the sight;
   glories stream from heaven afar,
   heavenly hosts sing Alleluia!
   Christ the Savior is born,
   Christ the Savior is born!

3. Silent night, holy night,
   Son of God, love's pure light;
   radiant beams from thy holy face
   with the dawn of redeeming grace,
   Jesus, Lord, at thy birth,
   Jesus, Lord, at thy birth.

4. Silent night, holy night,
   wondrous star, lend thy light;
   with the angels let us sing,
   Alleluia to our King;
   Christ the Savior is born,
   Christ the Savior is born!

Softly and Tenderly Jesus Is Calling

1. Softly and tenderly Jesus is calling,
   calling for you and for me;
   see, on the portals
   he's waiting and watching,
   watching for you and for me.
   Come home, come home;
   you who are weary, come home;
   earnestly, tenderly, Jesus is calling,
   calling, O sinner, come home!

2. Why should we tarry when Jesus is pleading,
   pleading for you and for me?
   Why should we linger
   and heed not his mercies,
   mercies for you and for me?
   Come home, come home;
   you who are weary, come home;
   earnestly, tenderly, Jesus is calling,
   calling, O sinner, come home!

3. O for the wonderful love he has promised,
   promised for you and for me!
   Though we have sinned,
   he has mercy and pardon,
   pardon for you and for me.
   Come home, come home;
   you who are weary, come home;
   earnestly, tenderly, Jesus is calling,
   calling, O sinner, come home!

Spirit of God, Descend Upon My Heart

1. Spirit of God, descend upon my heart;
   wean it from earth;
   through all its pulses move;
   stoop to my weakness, mighty as thou art,
   and make me love thee as I ought to love.

2. I ask no dream, no prophet ecstasies,
   no sudden rending of the veil of clay,
   no angel visitant, no opening skies;
   but take the dimness of my soul away.

3. Hast thou not bid me
   love thee, God and King?
   All, all thine own, soul,
   heart and strength and mind.
   I see thy cross; there teach my heart to cling.
   O let me seek thee, and O let me find!

4. Teach me to feel that thou art always nigh;
   teach me the struggles of the soul to bear.
   To check the rising doubt, the rebel sigh,
   teach me the patience of unanswered prayer.

5. Teach me to love thee as thine angels love,
   one holy passion filling all my frame;
   the kindling of the heaven-descended Dove,
   my heart an altar, and thy love the flame.

Stand Up, Stand Up for Jesus

1. Stand up, stand up for Jesus,
   ye soldiers of the cross;
   lift high his royal banner,
   it must not suffer loss.
   From victory unto victory
   his army shall he lead,
   till every foe is vanquished,
   and Christ is Lord indeed.

2. Stand up, stand up for Jesus,
   stand in his strength alone;
   the arm of flesh will fail you,
   ye dare not trust your own.
   Put on the gospel armor,
   each piece put on with prayer;
   where duty calls or danger,
   be never wanting there.

3. Stand up, stand up for Jesus,
   the strife will not be long;
   this day the noise of battle,
   the next the victor's song.
   To those who vanquish evil
   a crown of life shall be;
   they with the King of Glory
   shall reign eternally.

Standing on the Promises

1. Standing on the promises of Christ my King,
through eternal ages let his praises ring;
glory in the highest, I will shout and sing,
standing on the promises of God.
Standing, standing,
standing on the promises of God my Savior;
standing, standing,
I'm standing on the promises of God.

2. Standing on the promises that cannot fail,
when the howling storms of doubt
and fear assail,
by the living Word of God I shall prevail,
standing on the promises of God.
Standing, standing,
standing on the promises of God my Savior;
standing, standing,
I'm standing on the promises of God.

3. Standing on the promises I cannot fall,
listening every moment to the Spirit's call,
resting in my Savior as my all in all,
standing on the promises of God.
Standing, standing,
standing on the promises of God my Savior;
standing, standing,
I'm standing on the promises of God.

Sweet Hour of Prayer

1. Sweet hour of prayer! sweet hour of prayer!
   that calls me from a world of care,
   and bids me at my Father's throne
   make all my wants and wishes known.
   In seasons of distress and grief,
   my soul has often found relief,
   and oft escaped the tempter's snare
   by thy return, sweet hour of prayer!

2. Sweet hour of prayer! sweet hour of prayer!
   the joys I feel, the bliss I share
   of those whose anxious spirits burn
   with strong desires for thy return!
   With such I hasten to the place
   where God my Savior shows his face,
   and gladly take my station there,
   and wait for thee, sweet hour of prayer!

3. Sweet hour of prayer! sweet hour of prayer!
   thy wings shall my petition bear
   to him whose truth and faithfulness
   engage the waiting soul to bless.
   And since he bids me seek his face,
   believe his word, and trust his grace,
   I'll cast on him my every care,
   and wait for thee, sweet hour of prayer!

Take My Life, and Let It Be

1. Take my life, and let it be
   consecrated, Lord, to thee.
   Take my moments and my days;
   let them flow in ceaseless praise.
   Take my hands, and let them move
   at the impulse of thy love.
   Take my feet, and let them be
   swift and beautiful for thee.

2. Take my voice, and let me sing
   always, only, for my King.
   Take my lips, and let them be
   filled with messages from thee.
   Take my silver and my gold;
   not a mite would I withhold.
   Take my intellect, and use
   every power as thou shalt choose.

3. Take my will, and make it thine;
   it shall be no longer mine.
   Take my heart, it is thine own;
   it shall be thy royal throne.
   Take my love, my Lord, I pour
   at thy feet its treasure-store.
   Take myself, and I will be
   ever, only, all for thee.

Take Time to Be Holy

1. Take time to be holy, speak oft with thy Lord;
   abide in him always, and feed on his word.
   Make friends of God's children,
   help those who are weak,
   forgetting in nothing his blessing to seek.

2. Take time to be holy, the world rushes on;
   spend much time in secret with Jesus alone.
   By looking to Jesus, like him thou shalt be;
   thy friends in thy conduct
   his likeness shall see.

3. Take time to be holy, let him be thy guide,
   and run not before him, whatever betide.
   In joy or in sorrow, still follow the Lord,
   and, looking to Jesus, still trust in his word.

4. Take time to be holy, be calm in thy soul,
   each thought and each motive
   beneath his control.
   Thus led by his spirit to fountains of love,
   thou soon shalt be fitted for service above.

Tell Me the Stories of Jesus

1. Tell me the stories of Jesus
   I love to hear;
   things I would ask him to tell me
   if he were here:
   scenes by the wayside,
   tales of the sea,
   stories of Jesus,
   tell them to me.

2. First let me hear how the children
   stood round his knee,
   and I shall fancy his blessing
   resting on me;
   words full of kindness,
   deeds full of grace,
   all in the love-light
   of Jesus' face.

3. Into the city I'd follow
   the children's band,
   waving a branch of the palm tree
   high in my hand;
   one of his heralds,
   yes, I would sing
   loudest hosannas,
   "Jesus is King!"

The Battle Hymn of the Republic

1. Mine eyes have seen the glory
   of the coming of the Lord;
   he is trampling out the vintage
   where the grapes of wrath are stored;
   he hath loosed the fateful lightning
   of his terrible swift sword;
   his truth is marching on.
   Refrain
   Glory, glory, hallelujah!
   Glory, glory, hallelujah!
   Glory, glory, hallelujah!
   His truth is marching on.

2. He has sounded forth the trumpet
   that shall never call retreat;
   he is sifting out the hearts of men
   before his judgment seat;
   O be swift, my soul, to answer him;
   be jubilant, my feet!
   Our God is marching on. *Refrain*

3. In the beauty of the lilies
   Christ was born across the sea,
   with a glory in his bosom
   that transfigures you and me;
   as he died to make men holy,
   let us die to make men free,
   while God is marching on. *Refrain*

The Church's One Foundation

1. The church's one foundation
   is Jesus Christ her Lord;
   she is his new creation
   by water and the Word.
   From heaven he came and sought her
   to be his holy bride;
   with his own blood he bought her,
   and for her life he died.

2. Mid toil and tribulation,
   and tumult of her war,
   she waits the consummation
   of peace forevermore;
   till, with the vision glorious,
   her longing eyes are blest,
   and the great church victorious
   shall be the church at rest.

3. Yet she on earth hath union
   with God the Three in One,
   and mystic sweet communion
   with those whose rest is won.
   O happy ones and holy!
   Lord, give us grace that we
   like them, the meek and lowly,
   on high may dwell with thee.

The Day of Resurrection

1. The day of resurrection!
   Earth, tell it out abroad;
   the passover of gladness,
   the passover of God.
   From death to life eternal,
   from earth unto the sky,
   our Christ hath brought us over,
   with hymns of victory.

2. Our hearts be pure from evil,
   that we may see aright
   the Lord in rays eternal
   of resurrection light;
   and listening to his accents,
   may hear, so calm and plain,
   his own "All hail!" and, hearing,
   may raise the victor strain.

3. Now let the heavens be joyful!
   Let earth the song begin!
   Let the round world keep triumph,
   and all that is therein!
   Let all things seen and unseen
   their notes in gladness blend,
   for Christ the Lord hath risen,
   our joy that hath no end.

The Old Rugged Cross

1. On a hill far away stood an old rugged cross,
   the emblem of suffering and shame;
   and I love that old cross
   where the dearest and best
   for a world of lost sinners was slain.

   Refrain
   So I'll cherish the old rugged cross,
   till my trophies at last I lay down;
   I will cling to the old rugged cross,
   and exchange it some day for a crown.

2. O that old rugged cross,
   so despised by the world,
   has a wondrous attraction for me;
   for the dear Lamb of God left his glory above
   to bear it to dark Calvary. ***Refrain***

3. In that old rugged cross,
   stained with blood so divine,
   a wondrous beauty I see,
   for 'twas on that old cross
   Jesus suffered and died,
   to pardon and sanctify me. ***Refrain***

4. To the old rugged cross I will ever be true,
   its shame and reproach gladly bear;
   then he'll call me some day
   to my home far away,
   where his glory forever I'll share. ***Refrain***

There Is a Balm in Gilead

1. There is a balm in Gilead
   to make the wounded whole;
   there is a balm in Gilead
   to heal the sin-sick soul.
   Sometimes I feel discouraged,
   and think my work's in vain.
   But then the Holy Spirit
   revives my soul again.

2. There is a balm in Gilead
   to make the wounded whole;
   there is a balm in Gilead
   to heal the sin-sick soul.
   Don't ever feel discouraged,
   for Jesus is your friend,
   and if you look for knowledge
   he'll ne'er refuse to lend.

3. There is a balm in Gilead
   to make the wounded whole;
   there is a balm in Gilead
   to heal the sin-sick soul.
   If you can't preach like Peter,
   if you can't pray like Paul,
   just tell the love of Jesus,
   and say he died for all.

There Is a Fountain Filled With Blood

1. There is a fountain filled with blood
drawn from Emmanuel's veins;
and sinners plunged beneath that flood
lose all their guilty stains.
Lose all their guilty stains,
lose all their guilty stains;
and sinners plunged beneath that flood
lose all their guilty stains.

2. E'er since, by faith, I saw the stream
thy flowing wounds supply,
redeeming love has been my theme,
and shall be till I die.
And shall be till I die,
and shall be till I die;
redeeming love has been my theme,
and shall be till I die.

3. Then in a nobler, sweeter song,
I'll sing thy power to save,
when this poor lisping, stammering tongue
lies silent in the grave.
Lies silent in the grave,
lies silent in the grave;
when this poor lisping, stammering tongue
lies silent in the grave.

There's Within My Heart a Melody

1. There's within my heart a melody
   Jesus whispers sweet and low:
   Fear not, I am with thee, peace, be still,
   in all of life's ebb and flow.

   Refrain
   Jesus, Jesus, Jesus, sweetest name I know,
   fills my every longing, keeps me singing as I go.

2. All my life was wrecked by sin and strife,
   discord filled my heart with pain;
   Jesus swept across the broken strings,
   stirred the slumbering chords again. ***Refrain***

3. Though sometimes he leads
   through waters deep,
   trials fall across the way,
   though sometimes the path
   seems rough and steep,
   see his footprints all the way. ***Refrain***

4. Feasting on the riches of his grace,
   resting neath his sheltering wing,
   always looking on his smiling face,
   that is why I shout and sing. ***Refrain***

5. Soon he's coming back to welcome me
   far beyond the starry sky;
   I shall wing my flight to worlds unknown;
   I shall reign with him on high. ***Refrain***

This Is My Father's World

1. This is my Father's world,
   and to my listening ears
   all nature sings, and round me rings
   the music of the spheres.
   This is my Father's world:
   I rest me in the thought
   of rocks and trees, of skies and seas;
   his hand the wonders wrought.

2. This is my Father's world,
   the birds their carols raise,
   the morning light, the lily white,
   declare their maker's praise.
   This is my Father's world:
   he shines in all that's fair;
   in the rustling grass I hear him pass;
   he speaks to me everywhere.

3. This is my Father's world.
   O let me ne'er forget
   that though the wrong seems oft so strong,
   God is the ruler yet.
   This is my Father's world:
   why should my heart be sad?
   The Lord is King; let the heavens ring!
   God reigns; let the earth be glad!

'Tis So Sweet to Trust in Jesus

1. 'Tis so sweet to trust in Jesus,
   and to take him at his word;
   just to rest upon his promise,
   and to know, "Thus saith the Lord."

   Refrain
   Jesus, Jesus, how I trust him!
   How I've proved him o'er and o'er!
   Jesus, Jesus, precious Jesus!
   O for grace to trust him more!

2. O how sweet to trust in Jesus,
   just to trust his cleansing blood;
   and in simple faith to plunge me
   neath the healing, cleansing flood!
   Refrain

3. Yes, 'tis sweet to trust in Jesus,
   just from sin and self to cease;
   just from Jesus simply taking
   life and rest, and joy and peace.
   Refrain

4. I'm so glad I learned to trust thee,
   precious Jesus, Savior, friend;
   and I know that thou art with me,
   wilt be with me to the end.
   Refrain

To God Be the Glory

1. To God be the glory,
   great things he hath done!
   So loved he the world that he gave us his Son,
   who yielded his life an atonement for sin,
   and opened the life-gate that all may go in.

   Refrain
   Praise the Lord, praise the Lord,
   let the earth hear his voice!
   Praise the Lord, praise the Lord,
   let the people rejoice!
   O come to the Father
   thru Jesus the Son,
   and give him the glory,
   great things he hath done!

2. O perfect redemption, the purchase of blood,
   to every believer the promise of God;
   the vilest offender who truly believes,
   that moment from Jesus a pardon receives.
   Refrain

3. Great things he hath taught us,
   great things he hath done,
   and great our rejoicing thru Jesus the Son;
   but purer, and higher, and greater will be
   our wonder, our transport,
   when Jesus we see.
   Refrain

Turn Your Eyes Upon Jesus

Turn your eyes upon Jesus,
look full in his wonderful face,
and the things of earth will grow strangely dim
in the light of his glory and grace.

Up From the Grave He Arose

1. Low in the grave he lay, Jesus my Savior,
   waiting the coming day, Jesus my Lord!
   Up from the grave he arose,
   with a mighty triumph o'er his foes;
   he arose a victor from the dark domain,
   and he lives forever, with his saints to reign.
   He arose! He arose! Hallelujah! Christ arose!

2. Vainly they watch his bed, Jesus my Savior;
   vainly they seal the dead, Jesus my Lord!
   Up from the grave he arose,
   with a mighty triumph o'er his foes;
   he arose a victor from the dark domain,
   and he lives forever, with his saints to reign.
   He arose! He arose! Hallelujah! Christ arose!

3. Death cannot keep its prey, Jesus my Savior;
   he tore the bars away, Jesus my Lord!
   Up from the grave he arose,
   with a mighty triumph o'er his foes;
   he arose a victor from the dark domain,
   and he lives forever, with his saints to reign.
   He arose! He arose! Hallelujah! Christ arose!

We Gather Together

1. We gather together
   to ask the Lord's blessing;
   he chastens and hastens
   his will to make known.
   The wicked oppressing
   now cease from distressing.
   Sing praises to his name;
   he forgets not his own.

2. Beside us to guide us,
   our God with us joining,
   ordaining, maintaining
   his kingdom divine;
   so from the beginning
   the fight we were winning;
   thou, Lord, wast at our side,
   all glory be thine!

3. We all do extol thee,
   thou leader triumphant,
   and pray that thou still
   our defender wilt be.
   Let thy congregation
   escape tribulation;
   thy name be ever praised!
   O Lord, make us free!

Were You There

1. Were you there
when they crucified my Lord?
Were you there
when they crucified my Lord?
Oh! sometimes it causes me
to tremble, tremble, tremble.
Were you there
when they crucified my Lord?

2. Were you there
when they nailed him to the tree?
Were you there
when they nailed him to the tree?
Oh! sometimes it causes me
to tremble, tremble, tremble.
Were you there
when they nailed him to the tree?

3. Were you there
when they laid him in the tomb?
Were you there
when they laid him in the tomb?
Oh! sometimes it causes me
to tremble, tremble, tremble.
Were you there
when they laid him in the tomb?

What a Friend We Have in Jesus

1. What a friend we have in Jesus,
   all our sins and griefs to bear!
   What a privilege to carry
   everything to God in prayer!
   O what peace we often forfeit,
   O what needless pain we bear,
   all because we do not carry
   everything to God in prayer.

2. Have we trials and temptations?
   Is there trouble anywhere?
   We should never be discouraged;
   take it to the Lord in prayer.
   Can we find a friend so faithful
   who will all our sorrows share?
   Jesus knows our every weakness;
   take it to the Lord in prayer.

3. Are we weak and heavy laden,
   cumbered with a load of care?
   Precious Savior, still our refuge;
   take it to the Lord in prayer.
   Do thy friends despise, forsake thee?
   Take it to the Lord in prayer!
   In his arms he'll take and shield thee;
   thou wilt find a solace there.

What Child Is This

1. What child is this who, laid to rest,
   on Mary's lap is sleeping?
   Whom angels greet with anthems sweet,
   while shepherds watch are keeping?
   This, this is Christ the King,
   whom shepherds guard and angels sing;
   haste, haste to bring him laud,
   the babe, the son of Mary.

2. Why lies he in such mean estate
   where ox and ass are feeding?
   Good Christians, fear, for sinners here
   the silent Word is pleading.
   This, this is Christ the King,
   whom shepherds guard and angels sing;
   haste, haste to bring him laud,
   the babe, the son of Mary.

3. So bring him incense, gold, and myrrh,
   come, peasant, king, to own him;
   the King of kings salvation brings,
   let loving hearts enthrone him.
   This, this is Christ the King,
   whom shepherds guard and angels sing;
   haste, haste to bring him laud,
   the babe, the son of Mary.

When I Survey the Wondrous Cross

1. When I survey the wondrous cross
   on which the Prince of Glory died,
   my richest gain I count but loss,
   and pour contempt on all my pride.

2. Forbid it, Lord, that I should boast,
   save in the death of Christ, my God;
   all the vain things that charm me most,
   I sacrifice them to his blood.

3. See, from his head, his hands, his feet,
   sorrow and love flow mingled down.
   Did e'er such love and sorrow meet,
   or thorns compose so rich a crown?

4. Were the whole realm of nature mine,
   that were an offering far too small;
   love so amazing, so divine,
   demands my soul, my life, my all.

When We All Get to Heaven

1. Sing the wondrous love of Jesus;
   sing his mercy and his grace.
   In the mansions bright and blessed
   he'll prepare for us a place.
   When we all get to heaven,
   what a day of rejoicing that will be!
   When we all see Jesus,
   we'll sing and shout the victory!

2. While we walk the pilgrim pathway,
   clouds will overspread the sky;
   but when traveling days are over,
   not a shadow, not a sigh.
   When we all get to heaven,
   what a day of rejoicing that will be!
   When we all see Jesus,
   we'll sing and shout the victory!

3. Let us then be true and faithful,
   trusting, serving every day;
   just one glimpse of him in glory
   will the toils of life repay.
   When we all get to heaven,
   what a day of rejoicing that will be!
   When we all see Jesus,
   we'll sing and shout the victory!

Wonderful Words of Life

1. Sing them over again to me,
   wonderful words of life;
   let me more of their beauty see,
   wonderful words of life;
   words of life and beauty
   teach me faith and duty.

   Refrain
   Beautiful words, wonderful words,
   wonderful words of life.
   Beautiful words, wonderful words,
   wonderful words of life.

2. Christ, the blessed one, gives to all
   wonderful words of life;
   sinner, list to the loving call,
   wonderful words of life;
   all so freely given,
   wooing us to heaven.
   Refrain

3. Sweetly echo the gospel call,
   wonderful words of life;
   offer pardon and peace to all,
   wonderful words of life;
   Jesus, only Savior,
   sanctify forever.
   Refrain

Index

ROA: *Rock of Ages* (page in which song appears in this book)
UMH: *The United Methodist Hymnal* (The United Methodist Publishing House, 1989)
BH: *The Baptist Hymnal* (Convention Press, 1991)
PH: *The Presbyterian Hymnal* (Westminster/John Knox, 1990)
LBW: *Lutheran Book of Worship* (Augsburg Publishing House, 1978)

ROA		UMH	BH	PH	LBW
	EASTER				
44	Christ the Lord Is Risen Today	302	159	113	128
57	He Lives	310	533	-----	-----
108	The Day of Resurrection	303	164	118	141
117	Up From the Grave He Arose	322	160	-----	-----
	ADORATION AND PRAISE				
33	All Creatures of Our God and King	62	27	455	527
35	All Hail the Power of Jesus' Name	154	200	142	328
45	Come, Thou Almighty King	61	247	139	522
47	Crown Him With Many Crowns	327	161	151	170
50	For the Beauty of the Earth	92	44	473	561
69	Joyful, Joyful, We Adore Thee	89	7	464	551
75	Love Divine, All Loves Excelling	384	208	376	315
84	O for a Thousand Tongues to Sing	57	216	466	559
93	Praise to the Lord, the Almighty	139	14	482	543
	DEDICATION, CONSECRATION				
55	Have Thine Own Way, Lord	382	294	-----	-----
70	Just As I Am, Without One Plea	357	307	370	296
103	Take My Life, and Let It Be	399	283	-----	406
	PRAYER, TRUST, HOPE, GRACE, FAITH				
36	Amazing Grace	378	330	280	448
49	Faith of Our Fathers	710	352	-----	500
77	My Faith Looks Up to Thee	452	416	383	479
90	Onward, Christian Soldiers	575	493	-----	509
91	Open My Eyes, That I May See	454	502	324	-----
94	Rock of Ages, Cleft for Me	361	342	-----	327
102	Sweet Hour of Prayer	496	445	-----	-----
104	Take Time to Be Holy	395	446	-----	-----
118	We Gather Together	131	636	559	-----
	GOD/TRINITY				
30	A Mighty Fortress Is Our God	110	8	260	229
58	Holy, Holy, Holy! Lord God Almighty	64	2	138	165
81	Now Thank We All Our God	102	638	555	534
85	O God, Our Help in Ages Past	117	74	210	320

ROA		UMH	BH	PH	LBW
101	Standing on the Promises	374	335	-----	-----
113	This Is My Father's World	144	43	293	554
115	To God Be the Glory	98	4	485	-----
	JESUS CHRIST				
42	Blessed Assurance	369	334	341	-----
48	Fairest Lord Jesus	189	176	306	518
56	He Leadeth Me: O Blessed Thought	128	52	-----	501
59	How Firm a Foundation	529	338	361	507
61	I Love to Tell the Story	156	572	-----	390
63	In the Garden	314	187	-----	-----
67	Jesus Loves Me	191	344	304	-----
71	Leaning on the Everlasting Arms	133	333	-----	-----
78	My Hope Is Built	368	406	379	293
79	Near to the Heart of God	472	295	527	-----
86	O How I Love Jesus	170	217	-----	-----
87	O Jesus, I Have Promised	396	276	388	-----
92	Pass Me Not, O Gentle Savior	351	308	-----	-----
95	Savior, Like a Shepherd Lead Us	381	61	387	481
100	Stand Up, Stand Up for Jesus	514	485	-----	389
104	Take Time to Be Holy	395	446	-----	-----
105	Tell Me the Stories of Jesus	277	129	-----	-----
107	The Church's One Foundation	545	350	442	369
112	There's Within My Heart a Melody	380	425	-----	-----
114	'Tis So Sweet to Trust in Jesus	462	411	-----	-----
116	Turn Your Eyes Upon Jesus	349	320	-----	-----
120	What a Friend We Have in Jesus	526	182	403	439
	BIBLE				
67	Jesus Loves Me	191	344	304	-----
105	Tell Me the Stories of Jesus	277	129	-----	-----
124	Wonderful Words of Life	600	261	-----	-----
	HOLY SPIRIT				
43	Breathe on Me, Breath of God	420	241	316	488
99	Spirit of God, Descend Upon My Heart	500	245	326	486

ROA		UMH	BH	PH	LBW
	COMMUNION				
72	Let Us Break Bread Together	618	366	513	212
111	There Is a Fountain Filled With Blood	622	142	-----	-----
	COMFORT AND HEALING				
62	I Need Thee Every Hour	397	450	-----	-----
65	It Is Well With My Soul	377	410	-----	-----
80	Nearer, My God, to Thee	528	458	-----	-----
110	There Is a Balm in Gilead	375	269	394	-----
	ETERNAL LIFE (FUNERAL & MEMORIAL SERVICE)				
31	Abide With Me	700	63	543	272
52	God Be With You Till We Meet Again	672	-----	540	-----
76	Marching to Zion	733	524	-----	-----
80	Nearer, My God, to Thee	528	458	-----	-----
96	Shall We Gather at the River	723	518	-----	-----
98	Softly and Tenderly Jesus Is Calling	348	312	-----	-----
123	When We All Get to Heaven	701	514	-----	-----
	MARRIAGE				
89	O Perfect Love	645	512	533	287
	PATRIOTIC				
37	America (My Country, 'Tis of Thee)	697	634	561	566
38	America the Beautiful	696	630	564	-----
73	Lift Every Voice and Sing	519	627	563	562
106	The Battle Hymn of the Republic	717	633	-----	332
	SPIRITUALS				
51	Go, Tell It on the Mountain	251	95	29	70
72	Let Us Break Bread Together	618	366	513	212
110	There Is a Balm in Gilead	375	269	394	-----
119	Were You There	288	156	102	92